GROOMING SECRETS
FOR MEN

GROOMING SECRETS FOR MEN

THE ULTIMATE GUIDE TO LOOKING AND FEELING YOUR BEST

David Scott Bartky

iUniverse, Inc.
New York Bloomington Shanghai

GROOMING SECRETS FOR MEN
THE ULTIMATE GUIDE TO LOOKING AND FEELING YOUR BEST

Copyright © 2008 by David Sott Bartky

All rights reserved. No part of this book may be used or reproduced by any means, graphic, electronic, or mechanical, including photocopying, recording, taping or by any information storage retrieval system without the written permission of the publisher except in the case of brief quotations embodied in critical articles and reviews.

iUniverse books may be ordered through booksellers or by contacting:

iUniverse
1663 Liberty Drive
Bloomington, IN 47403
www.iuniverse.com
1-800-Authors (1-800-288-4677)

Because of the dynamic nature of the Internet, any Web addresses or links contained in this book may have changed since publication and may no longer be valid.

This book publication is being distributed with the expressed and implied understanding that the author and publisher are not engaged in rendering legal, accounting, medical or other professional advice. If legal advice is required, a competent professional should be sought. While the author has made every effort to be factual, based on research and a lifetime of experience, results may vary.

ISBN: 978-0-595-49311-1

Printed in the United States of America

Contents

INTRODUCTION vii
SKIN CARE 1
GIVE YOURSELF A FACIAL 12
BLACKHEAD REMOVAL 15
SKIN OF COLOR 18
SHAVING 21
BEARD MAINTENANCE 26
BODY HAIR 29
BODY ODOR 37
TOP FOUR GROOMING TIPS 40
SEX AND MEN'S GROOMING 41
HAIRPIECE/TOUPEE MAINTENANCE 44
OPTIONS FOR COLORING YOUR HAIR 47
HOW TO HAVE THICKER LOOKING HAIR 51
HEALTHY TEETH 53
FINDING YOUR OWN STYLE 56
WHAT TO WEAR 60
THE TRAVELING MAN 63
GROOMING TIPS WHILE ON A DATE 66

HOW TO LOOK YOUR BEST IN PHOTOGRAPHS 68
HOW TO WALK SO YOU LOOK YOUR BEST 71
EXERCISE and HEALTHY EATING 73
OTHER QUICK TIPS 81
CONCLUSION 89
HELPFUL LINKS AND BOOKS 91

INTRODUCTION

Congratulations! You are on your way to looking (and feeling) your best with these easy at home techniques. It's perfectly normal and natural for men to want to look their best. Looking your best not only makes you more attractive on the outside, it also gives you more self-confidence, which of course affects other areas of your life in a positive way. You're going to notice a positive difference in your appearance once you implement the techniques in *Grooming Secrets For Men*. Unlike women, most men don't go around talking about what they're doing to keep themselves looking great. Here is your opportunity to learn the secrets to looking and feeling your best. The best part is you can do it all from home!

A lot of guys feel it's not "masculine" to think about doing anything to improve their appearance outside of getting their hair cut. Unfortunately, somewhere along the line, men were left out of the loop when it came to "grooming" themselves to look their best. Times have changed! In this day and age, men's skin care products are flying off the shelves; men's salons and spas are booked to the hilt, etc. Obviously men want in on looking their best and so do you! This is your chance to find out how!

After reading, learning, and using the easy at home techniques in this book, you'll notice a positive, and sometimes even a dramatic difference in the way you look. I know this for a fact because I get emails from guys all over the world letting me know how much these techniques have helped them. Your friends and family will tell you how good you look (if they don't tell you, they're thinking it!) Get ready to enjoy the new you!

The good news is you can look YOUR best without spending a lot of time and money. "YOUR" best means just that! Not like the guy on the cover of that workout magazine, not like the guy in GQ, but YOUR best! That's what's important.

Try out all the ideas suggested in this book, or just the ones that appeal to you. Either way you'll find out a lot valuable information you can use your entire life, and have the "edge" over the rest, and you WILL look your best. Improving your appearance is guaranteed when you follow the advice only found here, in this book!

For those of you who haven't heard of me I have been passionate about men's grooming for the past 20 years! Over that span of time I've done my own research and sometimes even used myself as a "guinea pig" to figure out what works and what doesn't! Along the way I started giving advice to family and friends about grooming techniques they could do to improve their appearance and they saw great results! Sometimes strangers would even come up to me and ask me what I was doing to keep my skin looking so good! Eventually I realized that there was a need for this type of information so I decided to put it all in this book. I found out I was correct, *Grooming Secrets For Men* has sold all over the world!

I have written for many magazines such as *WWE Magazine* and *Ally Magazine*. I have also written many men's grooming related articles for various web sites and have written many articles regarding men's issues for www.mensflair.com and www.ezinearticles.com and have received very good ratings. Some of the skin care lines I have reviewed are: John Varvatos Skin, 4VOO Skin Care, Ice Elements, AboutFace4Men, Primal Skin Care, MaleFace, Task Essentials, Eminence Skin Care, and many more!

I also send out a monthly newsletter for my Grooming Club members. If you'd like to become a member of the Grooming Club, please go to my web site www.thestylishman.com, click on the "Grooming Club" tab and you'll be able to join so you can get the monthly Newsletter. The Newsletter is filled with men's grooming products reviews, style information and other topics pertaining to men's interests.

I'm glad you've decided to do something positive just for you. Doing what you can to look your best is very empowering. When you know you're doing what you can to look your best, you face the world every day with a more positive attitude. This positive attitude affects every area of your life for the better. What a win-win situation!

Let's get started on helping you look your best …

SKIN CARE

Let's face it (no pun intended) your face is your most important asset. It's what people notice first when they just see you, or meet you, or are talking to you. All day long your face is on display for everyone to see; it gets noticed! Therefore, keeping your skin as clean and clear as you can is ultra important. The first thing you must know is that there are a few basic skin types, and you have to figure out which one you are. So, which one of these skin types applies to you?

- DRY (tends to be flaky in certain areas and it feels dry and tight);
- NORMAL (not flaky, not shiny or oily, in the middle, feels comfortable);
- COMBINATION (oily forehead and/or nose, normal to dry cheeks)—**most guys have combination skin**; or
- OILY (shiny and oily all over, tends to break out and feels greasy, especially on your forehead and nose).

Right now, look in the mirror and try to figure out which type of skin you have. It's very important that you know which skin type applies to you as you'll learn a little later on.

In general, most men have combination or oily skin. Regardless of which type of skin you have, again, keeping it clean is a must. This means you must cleanse your skin morning and night with a face cleanser that is made for your particular skin type. Even at night, if you can't see the dirt and grime that's on your face when you get home from being out all day, it's there! Pollutants in the air mixed with the oils on your skin, equals clogged, dirty pores. Your pores need to be cleaned or else your skin will turn into skin that is irritated, which can cause pimples, blemishes and/or blackheads.

Skin care products for men and women fill the shelves at your local Sephora, drug store, mall, and on the Internet. The main things to remember when selecting products for yourself is that they should be fragrance free unless the fragrance is from natural ingredients (non-organic fragrances contain ingredients that can irritate the skin), are as natural as possible (again, chemicals can irritate skin as well as absorb into your system and cause reactions), and not tested on animals (there's no need to support companies who use and abuse animals for their testing when there's plenty of good choices available by companies who don't test their products on animals). Another reason to use natural products is that what you put on your skin absorbs into your system. Obviously, you don't want chemicals to absorb into your system, which could possibly cause allergies or other problems over time. You can tell if a product irritates your skin if your skin is red or blotchy after using it. If you start using a skin care product and you notice your skin is irritated, stop using it! Obviously something in the product is not in harmony with your system. Try something new until you find a product that works for your skin. A product that works for your skin will leave it calm and will improve your skin tone.

As far as which brand(s) to use, you must try it to know if you'll like it. Everyone's skin acts differently to skin care products. What works great for me may work great for your, or it may not work great for you. What works great for you, may not work great for your best friend, etc. Some skin care products say they are made specifically for men or for women. Don't concern yourself with that. You want the best product that works best for you. A product made for "men only", may work great for you. If it doesn't, don't be afraid to try another product that isn't made specifically for men. Research has shown that many skin care products (especially skin care companies that started making products only for women) that make products just for men, have the same ingredients as the women's products, but the manufacturer just puts a more masculine label on it! So, try what you will, but don't be afraid to try a product that claims it's made for women or comes in a flowery box! It may end up being the one that works best for your skin. Below I will let you know what type of products you should use daily.

Here's a helpful tip when you're on your hunt for skin care products. After you find the products that are appropriate for your skin type (normal, dry, combination or oily), here's a little secret that the stores don't want you to know about! Before you buy a full size bottle, ask the sales person if you can get a sample of the product. A sample size is usually the perfect amount to test a product to find out if it will work for you. If you can't get a sample size, find out if the store sells a travel size of whatever product(s) you want to try. If there is no other option but to buy a full sized bottle, jar or tube, make sure you can return or exchange the product if you don't like it. This is very important. This way, you can feel assured that after a few days, if you don't like the product, you can either get a store credit or your money back. The same goes for ordering products over the Internet. Sometimes they will send you a sample size for free! Of course, if you don't like a product, you should try something else until you do find something that agrees with your skin and that you do like. I keep repeating that because I really want you to like the product(s) you are using. Don't settle for products that don't work for your skin. Also, asking a store clerk what they recommend for your skin can work out just fine, but sometimes even they don't know what will work best for you. One thing they CAN do is to show you where you can find skin care products for your particular type of skin (dry, normal, combination, oily). The only way to truly know if a product is going to work for you is to try it for a few days and see. If you find you don't like it, return it and try something else. I promise, eventually you WILL find something you like that will improve your skin. For example, you will know you like a face cleanser if your skin improves and looks clearer after using it for a week. You will know if you like a face moisturizer if your skin absorbs the moisturizer without looking shiny or irritated, and it keeps your face free of dry flaky skin all day.

The very basic, quick skin care routine is this:

- Cleanse (morning and night);
- Moisturize (morning and night);
- Apply eye cream (morning and night); and
- Use a face scrub (2 to 3 times a week).

1. **Cleanse**. Morning and night use a face cleanser. A face cleanser removes the daily grime and pollution from your pores. Make sure you buy a face cleanser for your particular skin type. It will say on the label "For Oily Skin", "For Dry Skin", etc. The best way to use a cleanser is to first wash your hands. Then, saturate a washcloth with lukewarm water. Wring out the washcloth and wipe it across your face and neck getting the top layer of grime off your skin. Rinse the washcloth. Then, put a nickel size amount of face cleanser across the tips of your fingers. Add a little water to it and rub the tips of your fingers back and forth until a mild lather forms. (Different products create a thicker lather than others. A thin lather does not mean the product is not good, sometimes, products with a lot of lather to it contain chemicals that make it lather.) Then, apply the lather to your face and neck in a circular motion. Make sure to cleanse your forehead, nose, cheeks, chin and neck. Then take your washcloth and use it to rinse off all the cleanser. Do this TWO times. Washing off a cleanser two times assures you that it really is ALL off. You can use a washcloth to rinse the cleanser off, or you can use a round small face sponge, which you can find at any drug store. Either works well. You will actually see a difference in how your skin looks and feels when it is clean. It's softer to the touch, skin tone looks more even, and it will become clearer than it was if the product is working. In the morning it's easiest to use your face cleanser in the shower. You have to cleanse your face in the morning because at night your body detoxifies through your skin and it's important to cleanse off the toxins and oils that accumulated while you were sleeping.

2. **Moisturize**. After you have cleansed your face, apply a moisturizer that's made for your skin type both in the morning and in

the evening. You can apply the moisturizer even if your skin is a little damp after cleansing (you don't have to wait for your skin to be totally dry before applying your moisturizer). Even oily skin needs a good face moisturizer. Most people think if their skin is oily they don't have to moisturize. This is not true. A good moisturizer will actually help balance out the oil to make your skin less oily and shiny! When buying a moisturizer, again make sure it is suitable for your skin type. It will say on the label "For Combination Skin", "For Oily Skin", etc. It should also say "non-comedogenic" and "oil-free." This means it will not clog your pores and cause you to break out. You should also buy your day moisturizer with at least an SPF 15. There are some new theories out there suggesting that the reason why there is so much skin cancer is because we are using too much sunscreen, which in turn is making the skin even more sensitive to the sun. The people who are researching that issue suggest only using a sunscreen if you are going to sun bathe. In my opinion, I play it safe by using a moisturizer with an SPF of only 15 for during the day. Keep looking for more information regarding the use of an SPF as more research comes in. If you are going to sun bathe, use a stronger SPF. A 30 SPF is recommended when sun bathing or when you know you'll be in bright sun for a long time. (Make sure your moisturizer with sunscreen says that it protects against both UVA and UVB rays).

To use your moisturizer, apply a thin layer of moisturizer all over your face and neck. Take the time to make sure it is completely blended into the skin. If your moisturizer doesn't come in a tube and it comes in a jar, don't stick your fingers in the jar, it can contaminate the moisturizer. Instead of using your finger, use a plastic spatula that may have come with the product. If a plastic spatula doesn't come with the product, simply use a Q-Tip or small spoon to take out the moisturizer from the jar.

If you are going to sun bathe or know you will be outside in the sun for a while, don't forget to apply your moisturizer to the back of your neck and your ears. If you are balding or bald, make sure to cover that area with a moisturizer that has an SPF in it as well during the day to avoid burning your scalp.

One way to tell if a moisturizer is good for your particular skin is if it has a "light" feeling and isn't too shiny when applied. Having a shiny face is not appealing and can cause breakouts. If you try a moisturizer and your face looks red or shiny, return it and try another one that leaves your skin calm and with a more matte finish. A red face after applying moisturizer usually means it's irritating the skin. You may have a healthy glow, which is a good thing. That's different than having an irritated or shiny face. If you cleanse your skin when you get home after work (which is recommended), you should still use your day moisturizer, or you can purchase another moisturizer that doesn't have an SPF in it. You don't need an SPF at night. If you do decide to purchase a moisturizer without an SPF, again it should not leave your face red, irritated or shiny and should be as natural as possible. When applying your moisturizer at night, make sure to do it at least 30 minutes before going to sleep. This way it will have a chance to absorb into your skin and not onto your pillow!

3. **Apply eye cream**. Using a good eye cream is a must, even if you are under 30. A good eye cream will help reduce puffiness under the eye and help prevent wrinkles, especially the dreaded crow's feet. A good eye cream can sometimes even help hide the crow's feet that are already there. Apply the eye cream as part of your morning and

evening skin care routine. You can tell in a few days if the eye cream you are using is working. You WILL notice a difference if the bags under your eyes are less puffy and your crow's feet seem to be less noticeable. Once again, ask for a sample or make sure you can return it if you don't like it. With eye creams, a sample can last a long time since you only use a tiny bit under each eye. Simply apply a dot under each eye and gently, I repeat, GENTLY dab and blend the cream under each eye. Some eye creams can be applied above your eyelid as well. Some eye creams work so well that you will notice an immediate difference! If you don't have crow's feet because of your age, using an eye cream will help to prolong them from appearing.

4. **Use a face scrub**. One more step you must add to your skin care routine is using a face scrub. A face scrub only needs to be used a few times a week. Using a face scrub will slough off dead skin and leave your face smooth and refreshed. It can also help to remove blackheads that are on the surface of your skin. Here's how to use a face scrub. After you cleanse your skin, use a dime size amount of face scrub and GENTLY apply it to your face in an upward circular motion. Make sure to pay extra attention to your more oily areas such as your forehead and nose. Applying it with a lot of pressure will not make it work better and can damage your skin. After you use the scrub rinse it off thoroughly with a washcloth or small round sponge. It's a good idea to use the face scrub toward the end of your morning shower. The heat from the shower will open your pores and soften the skin, which makes it a great time to use your scrub. Your face scrub should also be made as natural and chemical free as possible. Make sure to check the ingredients. Keep in mind that when you are using a face scrub it shouldn't have large exfoliation

beads in it that have the potential to irritate the skin. A face scrub that's made with exfoliation beads that are ground very fine is better for the skin because it is gentle on the skin, yet still does the job. After using your face scrub, apply your moisturizer.

So, the order of your routine is to (i) cleanse, (ii) moisturize, (iii) apply your eye cream, and (iv) a few times a week, use a face scrub. For best results, use the face scrub in the shower after you cleanse your skin.

Finding the right products that work for your skin will make a huge improvement to how you look. Don't be lazy and keep a product that you don't think is working for you. Take the time to exchange it for something else. Sometimes a product will work great for you and then suddenly you find it's not working so great anymore after a few months. This can happen with skin care as your skin changes with time and can also change if you live in an area that has a change of seasons. For example, a moisturizer that works great in the winter may be too heavy to use in the summer. As soon as you find a product isn't work for you anymore, it's time to try something new.

Also, don't be afraid to use different brands for each product you use. You can try to use the same brand for your cleanser, moisturizer, eye cream and scrub, but realize that when you find a cleanser that you like, it doesn't mean that the moisturizer from the same line will work for you. You don't have to return the entire line, keep what works for you and try something else until you find the perfect combination for you.

Coming up, you will find a skin care chart. Use this chart to keep track of which products you are using. You may get lucky and really like the first product(s) you choose. However, if you're like me, it may take you trying several products before you find the right combination of skin care products that work great for you. Fill in the chart so you know which products you have already used and which products you like and don't like.

Even though I say that a skin care line that works for me may or may not work for you, I want to let you know about a few product lines to help you get started on your quest to finding quality products. They are: Ice Elements (www.iceelements.com), About Face 4 Men (www.aboutface4men.com), 4VOO (www.4VOO.com), and MaleFace (www.maleface.com). These products are all natural, innovative, for the most part very reasonably priced, and I have had good results with them, and you may too!

Once you find products that are keeping your skin looking great, make sure to tell your friends about them so they can also start on the road to looking their best. Men need to start sharing this information with their friends because they want to look their personal best too, even if they don't mention it!

One product I want to tell you about which will help control having oily, shiny looking skin is what's called "oil control blotting papers" or "shine control sheets." You can find these papers or sheets at Sephora, on-line, or at any beauty supply store. All you do is simply take a sheet and gently press it on your nose and/or forehead. Pull it away and you'll see it absorbed all the oil! Use these sheets a few times a day to help keep the oil under control. If you're bald, use one on your head too to help tame the oil and cut the shine.

Now that you know how to have fantastic looking skin there's no turning back! Investing the small amount of time it takes to keep your skin looking great will be one of the best investments in yourself you can make!

Here's the skin chart I was talking about:

TYPE OF PRODUCT (Cleanser, Moisturizer, Eye Cream, Scrub, Mask)	BRAND NAME	DATE FIRST USED	LIKE IT? (YES/NO)

GIVE YOURSELF A FACIAL

Once you get into taking care of your skin you'll want to try going to the next step. The next step would be to give yourself an at home facial. Of course, you can go to a salon and get a professional facial which is a great thing to do every once in a while. A professional facialist will be trained on how to extract deep blackheads and whiteheads, which are typically found on your nose (those little black or white dots that just won't go away), and also may have a good suggestion on what products to use. WARNING: Don't feel obligated to use the products a facialist suggests! They usually like to sell you the products they use. If you are already using something you like, stick with it! If you do try something recommended by a facialist, make sure you can return it if you don't like it!

However, this book is all about what you can do at home. So, to give yourself an at home facial, one product you will need that we haven't talked about yet is a facial mask. Depending on your skin type (dry, normal, combination or oily) at your local mall or on the

Internet, buy yourself a natural mask for your skin type. Typically for dry/normal skin you'll buy a moisturizing mask. For combination or oily skin you'll probably find a mask with clay in it. The clay pulls out the toxins from the skin and helps to normalize the oil. If you have oily skin don't over use a mask. Once a week is enough. Over use can trigger your skin to produce more oil.

Here are the basic steps to giving yourself a facial:

1. Clean your face and neck with your skin cleanser.

2. Then after cleansing, apply your mask. (Sometimes a mask will come in a tube and sometimes in a jar. If it comes in a jar it will most likely be sold with a mini spatula so that you don't have to stick your fingers in the jar. Putting your fingers in the jar can "contaminate" the product. If your mask doesn't come in a tube, ask the store if they have a mini-spatula. If they don't you can use a Q-Tip or spoon.) After you apply your mask, it will usually stay on for about 10—15 minutes, until it dries. (Check the label for the correct amount of time to leave it on).

3. After your mask stays on for the amount of time required, gently take a damp washcloth and first let the cloth sit on your face for a few seconds. The damp cloth will help moisten the mask so that it will be easier to remove. Then simply use your washcloth and remove the mask, rinsing the cloth in warm water every few seconds. When you think the mask is all off, wipe your face one more time with a clean washcloth. Sometimes residue from a mask is still on the skin even if you can't see it. When you do your final rinsing

of the skin, use cool water. This will help to close the pores and calm the skin.

4. When you are done cleaning your face of your mask, apply your moisturizer (taking your time to blend it in well). It's okay to apply your moisturizer even if your skin is a little damp. If you do a mask at night your moisturizer does not have to have an SPF in it. If you only have a day moisturizer just use that one.

5. Then, apply your eye cream by gently dabbing a few drops under each eye and gently blending it in.

Giving yourself a facial will leave your skin clean, refreshed and looking great. I recommend doing this at a minimum two times a month.

BLACKHEAD REMOVAL

One of the most troubling skin issues that men have are blackheads. Blackheads are little, tiny black dots mostly found on the nose, but can even be found on the forehead and cheeks. A blackhead is a plug of dry, dehydrated sebum (your skin's natural lubricant) that gets "stuck" in your pores on the way out of your skin. Some of the blackheads are on the surface of the skin, and some of them run deep. The good news is that even the deep blackheads can be removed—and from home!

You will need a few pieces of equipment to safely and easily remove the blackheads. First, you will need a steam machine for the face. I like the Moisturizing Mist Microdermabrasion System by Conair (from Bed Bath & Beyond). It's not expensive, and it comes with: the actual steam machine, and a battery operated face brush, which you can use for deep cleansing of the skin. You will also need a tool called a Blackhead Extractor. It is a small stainless steel wand (about four to five inches long) and has a loop at each end. Usually, one loop is bigger than the other. You can find a Blackhead Extractor on-line or at a local drugstore. The last thing you will need is a magnifying mirror. Magnifying mirrors come in different magnifying strengths. I suggest you get the 15X mirror. This will let you see your face 15 times closer than the human eye, which is important so you can see the blackheads up close when you extract them.

Here are the steps for blackhead removal. I suggest doing this at night before you go to sleep because your nose may be red for a few hours after the procedure. By the time you wake up in the morning, the redness should be gone. I also want to say that you have to be patient and be gentle with your skin. If a blackhead is stubborn and won't come out, you may need to go to a facialist to remove it. Don't over irritate the skin by over using the blackhead extractor. It may also hurt a little bit when you remove the blackheads; this is normal but the results are worth the pain!

Since the nose is the main area where blackheads are found, this example will be about removing them from the nose. First, you need to use your all-natural face cleanser and cleanse your skin. After cleansing your skin, steam your face for about 4-5 minutes with the face steamer. After steaming your face, look into the 15X mirror, and using your Blackhead Extractor gently put one end of the extractor on your nose and push down. As you push down you will see white "gook" pop out! This is a good sign! This is what you are trying to do—get all the gook out (the blackheads). Continue by gently moving the blackhead extractor in a small up and down motions while pressing down, and you will see the blackheads come out. After a few blackheads pop out, you will see the loop get full of gook. Quickly rinse off the loop of the debris, and continue cleaning out another section of your nose. Keep pressing down gently while moving the extractor around different sections of your nose (particularly the tip and sides of the nose).

After you think you are done removing the blackheads, rinse the extractor off and wash your face again to remove any excess debris. For your final rinse, use cool water. This will help close the pores that were opened by the steam.

Follow this procedure by using a natural facial toner (that is for your skin type) to help to soothe the area. Then, conclude the process by using your moisturizer. If you don't have a toner at home, simply use your moisturizer to help sooth the skin after the procedure.

Don't get frustrated the first time you try doing this. The more you practice doing the blackhead removal procedure, the easier it gets.

Your nose may look a little irritated after this procedure, but when the irritation calms down you will really like the results!

SKIN OF COLOR

The science of it all:

Certain skin problems are more common among men with darker skin tones.

To get very scientific, skin color is determined by cells called melanocytes. All races have the same number of these cells. Melanosomes are structures in the melanocytes that produce the pigment melanin. There are more and larger melanosomes in darker skin melanocytes than in those of lighter skin. Although men of color are better protected against skin cancer and premature wrinkling from sun exposure (lucky you), you should still consider using a good UVA/UVB sunscreen when you know you'll be out in the sun for a long period of time.

Darkening of the skin (a/k/a Post inflammatory Hyper pigmentation):

The darkening of the skin can sometimes occur after certain skin disorders such as acne or eczema. It can be common in all skin types but is more common and noticeable in darker skin. Early treatment can help prevent dark spots. Darkened areas of the skin could take months or even years to fade so be patient. Chemical peels; microdermabrasion and even bleaching medication prescribed by a licensed dermatologist can help fade the pigment faster. A chemical peel or microdermabrasion will also smooth your skin giving you a more youthful appearance. Avoid harsh scrubbing and abrasive treatments unless in your particular situation your dermatologist suggests it. A daily sunscreen on the area is important to prevent the area from becoming darker.

Vitiligo:

Vitiligo is a condition in which color loss appears on different areas of the skin on the face and sometimes the entire body can be affected. Most people with this condition do not regain skin color without treatment. Some methods used to help are cortisone or other creams, light treatments, laser treatments, intense pulsed light (IPL), or skin grafting may be used, but there doesn't seem to be a "perfect" therapy for this yet. A licensed dermatologist can suggest what treatment is best for you.

Dry or "Ashy Skin":

Dry or "ashy skin" can be a problem for guys in general, but may be especially distressing for guys with darker skin tones. It can produce a grayish "ashy" appearance. The regular use of a natural moisturizer can help, BUT if you develop pimples from the moisturizer either try another brand or see a dermatologist.

Now, if you have acne on your forehead and you use a pomade or hair oil, it may be from that. Make sure it is not spreading from your hair onto your forehead. There should be about an inch of space from the hairline to the forehead. Make sure to clean your skin at the end of the day so that any excess oil will be washed off and not allowed to cause irritation.

Razor Bumps:

Razor bumps are the most common "problem" with men of color. What happens is that the hair shafts are curved and curly instead of straight. After shaving, especially after a close shave, the beard's sharp pointed hair may grow back into the skin. This causes the "bump."

One way to avoid this problem is to grow a beard. Also, shaving with a safety razor may help. After applying lather or shaving cream, wait to let the soap soften the beard and shave only in the direction of the hair growth, not against the stubble. Remember, DON'T STRETCH the skin during shaving and try not to shave every day. Lift up the hairs that begin to become ingrown with an alcohol cleansed needle or tweezers (do NOT pluck) just before shaving. Lifting the hair will help the razor cut it instead of pushing it into the skin.

Occasionally, the use of a toothbrush or rough washcloth before shaving may loosen the hairs that are about to grow inward. If you use a chemical depilatory, only use it every two days and they must be wiped off immediately according to the directions. Wash your face twice with your facial cleanser directly after to guard against irritation.

Some other options are laser hair removal and there are medicated creams that can be used to slow the hair growth. Your dermatologist can guide you on which treatment to try.

Also, using an aloe vera cream and/or a vitamin E cream may also help keep the skin healthy, and less irritated.

SHAVING

The dreaded morning shave doesn't have to be a horrible chore! We all know that shaving the face is one of those things that men have to do, but don't necessarily like doing. Even so, unless you have a beard, shaving is a part of your morning routine! Obviously, there are different ways to shave. The most common way to shave is by using a disposable razor or a safety razor. Either method works, but using a safety razor will give you a smoother, less irritating, less bumpy shave. With either method there is something you should ALWAYS do when shaving. Use a shaving brush! That's right, using a shaving brush will improve your shave big time. A good shaving brush exfoliates the skin and lifts the beard, which prepares your beard for a smoother shave. Of course there are different types of shaving brushes in all price ranges. I have found that even an inexpensive shaving brush works great as long as it's made with real badger hair, NOT synthetic hair. Synthetic hair will irritate your skin, which is the last thing you want! (There are a few companies coming out with synthetic shaving brushes that they claim work just as good or even "better" than badger hair. If you come across one of these new brushes, feel free to give it a try but make sure you can return it if it irritates your skin.)

Now here's the trick. You have to do what's called a "wet shave." A wet shave is done usually just after your morning shower while the beard is moist and soft. Using warm to hot (but not scalding) water, take a washcloth and let the warm water penetrate the cloth. Wring out the washcloth so it is damp. Then hold it over your face and neck to moisten the area. Then take your shave brush and moisten it for a minute with warm water, suds up either a shaving soap or cream with the brush, and apply the shaving soap or cream in a circular motion all over the area to be shaved. After you have worked up a good lather, shave in the direction in which the hair grows. You have to actually feel the stubble on your beard to find out which direction the hair is growing in. If you have a heavy beard you may need to dampen the washcloth again with warm/hot water and wet your face again. Using the brush, soap up your face again and gently shave against the grain. If you choose to try a safety razor (which I highly recommend if you are not already using one—you will get a closer shave), or are already using a safety razor, the trick to getting a great shave with a safety razor is DON'T PUSH DOWN against the skin when shaving. Let it gently glide across the beard, using its own weight for pressure. Using a safety razor is not like using a disposable razor in the sense that when you use a disposable razor you have to push down to get a close shave. When using a safety razor the blade is much sharper so pushing down will be too harsh for the skin. You simply let the weight of the razor guide the blade, which ends up leaving you with a very close smooth shave. Practice makes perfect when it comes to using a safety razor, and the results are worth the practice.

When you are done with your shave, take your washcloth and run it under cold water and wash your face off with the cold washcloth. The cold water will close the pores and help sooth the freshly shaved skin. After you have shaved, chances are there will be some irritation. Using a good aftershave, preferably one that has rose water or aloe in it will sooth and calm the skin. Your skin should NOT be irritated and burning after you use an aftershave. If it does burn, STOP using that product and try another one that actually soothes the skin! A fragrance free, gentle after-shave usually will not burn or sting. If your skin is very irritated when you are done shaving, you can try using a shaving oil under your shave cream. Shaving oil can help you attain a smoother, less irritating shave. You can try using shaving oil, but if you find it didn't make much of a difference, try a different shaving soap or cream until you find one that leaves your skin less irritated. If you haven't tried using a shaving soap with a shaving brush you're missing out on what could be your best shave. It's amazing what a difference the "right" shaving cream/soap makes. You may have to try several before finding the one that works best for you. Another great option for getting a less irritating shave is to spray a spray moisturizer on the skin after you let the warm washcloth saturate the skin. You can find a moisture spray from many of the top skin care lines such as Clinique and Task Essentials. Some of the moisture sprays even have aloe and vitamin E in them for further lubrication. Using a moisture spray before applying your shaving cream or soap will give the skin an even thicker cushion of moisture so the blade will glide over it easier, thus leaving you with much less irritated skin.

One item I do recommend using after you shave is what's called an Allum Block. An Allum Block is a somewhat clear block that you can find at a higher end shaving shop (although they only cost about $15). The Allum Block has natural antiseptic properties, which help calm the skin AFTER shaving and help stop little nicks from bleeding. The way to use the Allum Block is after you're done with your shave, wet the block with cold water and rub it all over your skin. You can even rub it on your cheeks, nose and forehead, which can help keep your skin clear. An Allum Block does wonders for freshly shaved skin by calming it and stopping any small nicks from bleeding.

If you are totally clean-shaven, or you shave your mustache area, make sure to shave the area just below your nose. For some reason lots of guys either think people won't notice that area, they're afraid to go there with their razor, or they're not aware that they forget to shave in that spot. People DO notice that you forgot to shave that one spot and it doesn't look good. It can be tricky to get it totally smooth, but do your best by gently using your razor up to the bottom of the nose. You can even lift the tip of your nose to expose the area, which will make it easier for you to shave in that spot. If there are still a few hairs directly under your nose that you can't get with your razor, use a small safety scissor to trim them down.

Electric Razors:

Although an electric razor can be easier to use, I don't recommend using an electric razor. An electric razor can tend to stretch the skin, and over time leave you with sagging skin. Most guys when using an electric razor pull the skin up or down so that the razor glides across it more easily, and to raise the hairs so the razor can trim them. Many electric razors will tell you in the directions to stretch the skin to get a closer shave. Doing this day after day, year after year may leave you with sagging skin, or "jowls." For this reason, I first recommend a wet shave with a safety razor, or in second place, a disposable razor. However, if you do decide to use an electric razor try using a pre-shave made specifically for use with an electric razor. This will help the blades to more gently glide across your skin, leaving your skin less irritated. When using an electric razor on your neck, to shave your neck as smooth as possible, don't just go in an up and down motion; gently glide the electric razor across your neck from left to right. This will more easily cut those stubborn hairs that won't cut in the up and down motion. Of course, if you do use an electric razor DON'T STRETCH YOUR SKIN or you'll be left with sagging skin at your jaw line! When you think you're done using your electric razor, quickly glide your fingers over your face and neck to check for any stubble you may have missed. If you find any, of course glide over it gently going against the grain with the razor for a perfect shave. After you are done using your electric razor, as with the wet shave, apply a cold washcloth to your face and neck to help sooth the freshly shaved skin. Follow that by using a soothing after-shave to help calm the skin.

BEARD MAINTENANCE

Whether you already have a beard or are thinking of growing one there are a few basic grooming tips you need to know about. If you are just starting to grow a beard you have to start shaping it from the beginning. Typically you would only shave the parts of the face and neck that you want to keep clean shaven (i.e., just below the cheek bones on the face, and the lower part of your neck). As the beard grows in, keep defining the shape of it until you find you're happy with the look you're going for. As the beard is growing in make sure to trim any long, scraggly hairs to keep it looking well groomed. To do this you'll need a fine tooth comb and a pair of barber's scissors for the most precise cut. Simply take the comb and comb down a section of the beard. The longer beard hairs will fall on the outside of the teeth of the comb, these hairs that are too long simply cut with your scissors. Go through the entire beard using this technique to keep its shape looking great.

If you want to consistently have the "just grown in" look get yourself a beard trimmer. Philips, Norelco, Panasonic and Wahl all make very good ones. The more recent models even have a vacuum system that catches the trimmed hairs so that they don't end up all over the floor! Using the beard trimmer on the lowest setting will give you this look. Of course you still have to shave the areas on your face and neck to give it the shape you desire.

Here are some more tips you must know about. First of all you must shampoo and condition your beard. This will keep your beard clean and soft. Make sure to thoroughly rinse out all the conditioner. If you don't, your skin can get itchy and flaky. You can find specific shampoos and conditioners made just for beards. They will typically not have any ingredients that will leave your skin itchy after use, as compared to using a regular shampoo or conditioner. A few product lines that make shampoos and conditioners specifically for beards are Bluebeard's shampoo called "Original Beard Wash", and Beardsly makes products called Ultra Beard Shampoo and Conditioner that will help keep your beard clean and soft.

After your beard is shampooed and conditioned, towel dry it and add a product that has shea butter in it. Shea butter will help keep the skin conditioned and the beard soft throughout the day. Another good option would be to gently rub in some organic olive oil into the skin and beard. This will also keep the skin from itching and the beard nice and soft. A little goes a long way so don't overuse the olive oil.

Some guys like to keep their beard from going gray. If that's you, you can easily color your beard. Go for an all-natural beard coloring system like the one from WolfsHead. It comes in six different colors so there's sure to be the right one for you. Their beard color is henna-based, natural, and hypoallergenic and contains no irritating chemicals. It comes in a two-ounce jar, which is good for multiple applications for those with normal sized beards (and mustaches). Included in the package are a beard comb, an applicator brush, and a set of complete, simple instructions. Unlike harsh chemical treatments you can apply a natural dye like WolfsHead whenever and as often as you decide. Typically you'll have to apply the color weekly for the first month or so, and then every other week once you get the desired color. The other good thing is that it doesn't require any mixing since it's a natural product.

Also, remember to always check your beard after eating to make sure no food or drink debris is in the hair. We've all seen guys walking around with crumbs of food stuck in their beards. Don't let that be you! Just take a few seconds and look in the mirror to check or simply brush your beard off with your fingers to clear if of crumbs!

BODY HAIR

Most men have body hair. Some of us like it and some of us would like to take a magic pill to rid ourselves of body hair. Since there's no magic pill you have to take matters into your own hands. Fortunately for those of you who want less body hair, the good news is it is possible to tame. Body hair consists of nose hair, ear hair, eyebrow hair, the hair between your eyebrows, back hair, and all other hair that grows on the body. Sometimes we just don't want it!

When it comes to body hair, certain areas of the body should be checked at least every other day (for example, nose hairs, ear hairs, hair between the eye brows, eyebrows, and neck hair).

Nose Hair:

Ok guys look in the mirror. Do you have hairs coming out of your nose? If so, no one wants to see them! When you talk to someone face-to-face, the person you're talking to will focus in on them and think to themselves how unappealing it looks! Taking the time to trim them will make you more appealing for sure. There are a few techniques to trimming nose hairs. One way is to use a small safety scissor that you can buy at any drug store. Gently and carefully take the scissor and cut around the perimeter of each nostril. You don't have to go inside the nostril very deep. You just want to cut the hair that is sticking out. You can also push up the tip of your nose, which will expose more hair that needs trimming. You can also purchase one of those fancy nose hair trimmers, but using a safety scissor is just as easy and I find works better. If you have very wide nostrils, your nose hairs will be easier to see, so make sure to take the time to trim whatever hair is sticking out. Doing this is a must!

Hair on the outside of the nose:

Most guys don't know about this one, but hairs on the outside of the nose can be, and usually are there. Hair on the outside of the nose is very common. It can most commonly be found on the tip and sides of the nose. Sometimes they can be long and sometimes just little sprouts sticking out. Now that you are aware they ARE there, go to the mirror and see if you can see any. For the longer hairs just pluck them with tweezers. Another easy way to rid the outside of your nose of hairs is to use one of the many nose strips that you can find at your local drug store. I personally like the Biore nose strips. The way most of these strips work is you have to wet the outside of your nose, pull off the strip from it's package, and place it on your damp nose for about 10 minutes until it dries. Once it is dry, you gently pull it off and you'll be amazed at what you see. Lots of little hairs and possibly some blackheads that were just at the surface of your nose will be on the strip. You should only use the strips once every few weeks. If you don't see any hairs on the outside of your nose it doesn't mean they're not there. After using a nose strip, you'll see them!

Ear Hair:

Another area you must pay attention to is ear hair. Ear hair grows out from many places of the ear. There is hair that comes out from the center of the ear, the lobe of the ear and the perimeter of the ear. All these areas must be checked and if needed the hair trimmed. There are several ways to trim these hairs. One way is to use your safety scissors and trim all the noticeable hairs growing out of the center of the ear. Then check the lobe and trim hairs from the lobe area. To trim the perimeter of the ear you can use your safety scissors, or if you have any type of electric razor, simply go over the ear with the razor. Keep your ears hair free!

Eyebrows:

Keeping your eyebrows trimmed is something that most guys don't think about. Sometimes your barber will think about it for you and trim them. But you can't rely on that because eyebrows need to be trimmed on a regular basis. Unless you're going for the bushy eyebrow look a few simple at home techniques can be performed. The easiest way to trim the eyebrow hair is to use your index finger and push up a section of the eyebrow. All the long hairs will rise above the tip of your finger. Those are the hairs that need to be trimmed. Simply use your safety scissors and trim the hairs that rise above your finger. Then go to the next section of the eyebrow and repeat the same thing until the entire brow is trimmed. Then move on to the other eyebrow doing the same. You will notice a wonderful difference.

Another technique you can use involves a standard hair comb. Using the part of the comb where the teeth are very close together, comb a section of the eyebrow up and slightly against the growth of the hair. If your right eyebrow hair naturally grows to the right, use the comb and lift the hair and gently tilt the comb to the left. All the long hairs will rise up above the teeth of the comb. Take your safety scissor and trim the hairs that are on the outside of the comb. Repeat this procedure all along the eyebrow and you will have a wonderful looking brow. Practice makes perfect when it comes to trimming your eyebrows. What a wonderful difference you will notice. You will not only look younger, you will have a much "cleaner" look. Try it; you'll like how it looks!

Hair between your eyebrows:

Lots of us have hair between the eyebrows. Typically, most guys don't want it there. To get rid of the hair between the brows, go buy yourself good pair of all-purpose tweezers. Using your tweezers, pluck the center hairs, about a half inch space. Don't overdo it. A good idea is to find a picture of a guy in a magazine that doesn't have any hair between the brows. See how big the gap between the brows is and that should give you an idea of how much to pluck. Another way you can get rid of those hairs is by using an electric sideburn or beard trimmer that has a narrow head on it. You can simply run it along the area where the hair is and trim it. Although it won't last as long as tweezing the hair will, it is a good alternative. One tip you should know about is that if you pluck the hairs between your eyebrows after a hot shower, the hairs will be easier to remove, as the heat from the shower will soften them.

Neck Hair:

I know the barber trims your neck hair but it starts growing and showing again within just a few days. When you let your neck hair grow too much, it just looks like you don't pay attention to your looks, and it looks very sloppy. The easiest way to keep your neck hair trimmed is by using an electric razor. Using an electric razor and a mirror held behind your head, trim the hair from the hairline down to the upper part of the back. After a while you won't need a mirror because you'll get the feel of where to trim. Keeping a clean neck makes you look cleaner, and more "with it." It's one of those areas that when kept clean, makes a big difference in how you look. If you let your neck hair get too long and then decide to trim it, use a sideburn trimmer on your electric razor to first trim the hairs down and then use the electric razor to smooth out the area.

Like keeping your eyebrows, nose, and ear hairs under control, keeping your neck hair under control is just as important and you and your friends will notice an improvement in your looks. Your friends won't know exactly why you look better, but they will think it!

Back Hair:

Most men have back hair. Most men don't want it! Back hair is a common annoyance for most men. Fortunately there are ways to remove it at home. The best at home technique to removing back hair requires a spouse or best friend! You'll need to purchase one of those hair-grooming tools usually called a hair trimmer, beard trimmer, or electric cutting sheers. I personally like the one called "The Peanut" by Wahl. Most cutting shears come with about four blade covers, each one with longer teeth than the other. Sometimes the blade covers are numbered 1—4, 1 being the cover with the shortest teeth and 4 being the cover with the longest teeth. For trimming your back you're going to want to start by using the blade cover that has the shortest teeth. This is usually called the "blending" cover. If your set doesn't have a "blending" cover, use the #1 cover. Have your friend trim your back hair using the hair trimmer by going against the grain of the hair. The hair usually grows in all different directions so it has to be trimmed from all directions. Once your hair is trimmed to a very low stub, you can then have your friend take off the blade cover and just use the blade. Gently glide the blade across the skin in different directions to really cut the hair close to the skin. When done, your back will be very smooth and look great. If you want to get the hair cut down even more, have your friend use an electric razor as the finishing touch that will make your back baby smooth! This step isn't necessary, but if you can do it, it's worth the extra few minutes.

It's good to follow this technique by having your friend apply a body moisturizer to your skin to soothe the skin. Depending on how fast your hair grows; this technique will most likely have to be repeated every four weeks to keep the back smooth. You can also buy an at-home waxing kit. The kit usually involves heating up a wax, applying the wax with a wood strip, and then applying a soft cloth to the wax, followed by pulling up the cloth which pulls the hair out at the same time. It can be painful and irritate the skin, so I would recommend the other option.

Body Hair Trimming:

If you are very hairy all over, or have hair on a particular part of your body (chest, arms, legs, butt, etc.), and have always wondered what it would look like and feel like to have less body hair, use the same cutting sheers you used on your back. (Again, "The Peanut" by Wahl works great for this). The only difference is you'll want to start by using the blade cover that has the longest teeth. After you put on the blade cover with the longest teeth, start by trimming your legs. This is best done by standing in your bathtub so that when you're done it's easy to clean up the hair. Make sure to use the sheers in all different directions as the hair grows in all different directions. Once you have trimmed your legs, if you think you may want to go shorter, try trimming them with the blade cover that's a little shorter than the one you just used. (For example, if you just used a number 4 blade cover, try using the number 3 blade cover). You're going to have to experiment to see which blade cover to use. Remember, you want to have a natural look, not a look that says, "I just trimmed my legs (arms, chest, etc.)!" You will know when you have a natural look when you look like you have less hair, but enough where it looks like you didn't do anything. That's the trick, and the only way to know when to stop is by trying each level of blade covers until you determine which one gives you that natural look. Once you figure out which blade covers work best for you then from then on you'll be able to trim in a matter of minutes.

If you are going to trim your chest and you have a very hairy chest, make sure to leave a few stragglers at your neckline or else it will look too perfect and can look like you're wearing a hair shirt! If you just have a patch of hair on your chest, you can use your trimming shears to trim it as close to the skin as possible, and then you can use your regular razor to shave off the excess until smooth.

Trimming/Shaving your "privates":

Lots of guys want to have trimmed pubic hair and clean shaven balls. This can easily be accomplished. Usually to trim your pubic hair you'll again use your electric hair trimmer/sheers (the Peanut by

Wahl once again works great in this area too). Again, you'll have to practice by trying the different size blade covers until you accomplish the look you are going for. If you want to trim your balls, use the blade cover with the shortest teeth to get the smoothest look. Remember; be VERY gentle when trimming your balls. Even though the blade cover is on, if you're not careful you can cut yourself. You can also try shaving your balls with a disposable razor. This is best accomplished by shaving them in the shower. When wet, apply either soap or shaving cream to your balls. Then, gently use a disposable razor and start shaving. This will take practice, but when you get the knack, you'll be an expert! If your skin still gets cut, you can purchase a shaving oil which may help protect the skin even further from the razor and give you a smoother shave. Shaving your balls with baby oil can also give you a smooth shave. Simply apply baby oil all over the area and gently shave. In general, be very gentle when shaving that area and in time you will figure out which technique works best for you. Once you shave them, keep them shaved every few days in the shower to prevent the hair from growing too long. The shorter the hair, the easier it is to shave.

BODY ODOR

This is one of the best pieces of information that you will find out about when it comes to smelling good and never having to worry about body odor ("B.O."). I have tried so many natural underarm deodorants and I just wasn't satisfied with the results. No matter how much I used, half way through the day I didn't like the smell. We all have experienced B.O. at one time or another. Some guys also experience it coming from their crotch. B.O. is actually not coming from your sweat directly. The reason for the B.O. is that the sweat contains a substantial amount of oil, which provides food for bacteria. It's the bacteria feeding on the sweat that creates the odor. The amazing news is that there is a way to eliminate B.O. all day long, and naturally!

I always remind guys to only use an all-natural underarm deodorant because what you put on your skin absorbs into your system. Most underarm deodorants are made with harsh chemicals and you don't want those absorbing into your system day after day (not to mention they can irritate the sensitive skin under your arms). If you're not happy with the results of trying an all-natural deodorant, or if you want to try an amazing homemade, all natural one, here is what you can do.

If you don't have one at home, go to a drugstore and buy a small spray bottle. Then, go to your local health food store and buy a bottle of organic distilled white vinegar and a bottle of pure water—this is the magic formula! Fill your spray bottle with 50% distilled white vinegar, and 50% pure water. Shake the bottle and then spray under your arms after showering. For a few minutes you will smell the vinegar but it will dissipate. If it's too strong for you, change the formula to 40% vinegar/60% pure water. You can also add a small amount of lavender or peppermint oil to the mixture to give it a nice scent. This formula works so well you may never go back to store bought deodorants! If you have a smelly crotch, you can also spray it there as well. I use this formula myself under my arms and am extremely happy with the results, no more B.O.! Even after sweating it will still keep you odor free! How amazing is that! If you find at some point during the day you do smell B.O., simply spray again and it will kill the odor. Another plan that works well for guys is that they first use the distilled vinegar/water spray and then follow it with their all natural under arm deodorant. This will give you double protection against B.O.!

Another good remedy for controlling B.O. is to mix a teaspoon of chlorophyll to a cup of water a few times a day. You can buy chlorophyll at your local health food store. After a few days this should cut down or eliminate the B.O.!

There is one natural under arm deodorant that works extremely well. Out of all the natural deodorants I have tried this is the only one that really works. The box says that one application will keep odor away for up to 7 days. I have found one application lasts for 5 days, which is still excellent. The product is called Lavilin. It's a cream deodorant. For the first application, after not using a deodorant for two days, you simply apply the cream under each arm after showering. You don't have to apply it again for a week! I highly recommend this product. The only downside to it is that it is expensive as far as under arm deodorants go, but well worth the price due to the great results.

Give these remedies a try and you'll be doing your body, and the people you come in contact with, a favor!

TOP FOUR GROOMING TIPS

HERE ARE THE TOP FOUR GROOMING TIPS THAT YOU MUST DO BEFORE EVER LEAVING YOUR HOUSE!!!!!

1. **Check your nose hairs**—trim them if they need to be trimmed.

2. **Check your ear hairs**—trim all ear hair if they need to be trimmed.

3. **Check your neck hair**—trim your neck hairs if they need to be trimmed.

4. **Check your eyebrows**—if your eyebrows are too bushy trim them! This will make a huge difference.

The "Top Four" are simple to check, easy to remedy, and worth their weight in gold due to the improvement in your appearance they make, which makes them the Top Four!!!

Take the few minutes it takes to check them and leave your home with full confidence that you look your best!!!

SEX AND MEN'S GROOMING

You may wonder what men's grooming has to do with sex! The truth is it has a lot to do with it! First of all, just by following the advice in this book and keeping yourself well groomed and looking your personal best WILL guarantee that you're more attractive and as a result, more sexually appealing. You'll also be more confident because you know you look your personal best. This confidence helps in all areas of your life, including in the bedroom!

There are a few grooming issues you need to think about when it comes to sex. Keeping your crotch well groomed is a must. Make sure to keep your pubic hair trimmed so that you don't have too much "bush" going on. This just makes the crotch look better and more sex ready! Another advantage to keeping your pubic hair trimmed is a lot of guys want their penis to look bigger. If you want to make your penis look bigger, keeping your pubic hair to a minimum makes it look bigger because more is exposed, rather than hiding in the "bush."

You also want to make sure that you don't have crotch odor. No one likes to smell a musty smelling crotch. There are several options to remedy crotch odor. First of all, if you can, shower before you have sex. Showering even a few hours before sex will help eliminate crotch odor. Another option would be to use your natural under arm deodorant between your thighs. This will keep the area smelling good and help to prevent odor. Of course I know you'll use an all-natural deodorant so you don't have to worry about irritation. You can also use the all-natural remedy I suggested in the "Body Odor" chapter. Just spray it between your thighs and this will also keep the area smelling good.

Speaking about body odor, this is another area you want to make sure is under control. Smell your underarms and make sure you don't have B.O. If you do have B.O. and you don't want to shower either re-use your natural underarm deodorant or spray the natural B.O. spray that I referred to earlier in the book. You can also assure you smell great by using cologne. I like all natural cologne like the one from Herban Cowboy called Dusk. It's organic cologne that smells great. Whatever cologne you use, make sure not to over use it. Just spray a little on yourself so just a hint of it comes through. If you over use cologne, it could irritate the person you're with and that's the last thing you want to do! If you're allergic to cologne or your partner is, using an all-natural scented body moisturizer would also make you smell very appealing.

Since we covered body odor, what about bad breath? If you've just had dinner or haven't brushed your teeth for several hours don't even think about kissing someone! Make sure to carry natural breath mints or gum on you so that your breath will be a turn on, instead of a turn off!

Another way to make yourself look more appealing in the bedroom is to wear sexy underwear. Wearing sexy underwear can be a huge turn on. The trick to this is that you have to wear underwear that will be appealing on your particular body type. If you're in great shape, wearing bikini or form fitting underwear will make you even sexier. However, if you're not in particularly good shape or even overweight, make sure to wear a pair of underwear that flatters your body type. Typically boxer briefs will be more flattering on someone who's not in great shape than bikini style underwear. You also need to think about what color your underwear is. White can be sexy, but also try something different like red or black. You can also find underwear that has mesh on the sides or mesh everywhere. Underwear for men is a big industry and there are so many unusual and sexy styles to choose from. Step out of your comfort zone and try a pair of underwear that is different from the regular briefs. There are so many on-line underwear shops (internationaljock.com, topdrawers.com, etc.) check them out and give something different a try.

Now that you know how to look your best in the bedroom, you'll be more confident and sexier, so you and your partner will both benefit from your awareness of looking your best in the bedroom!

HAIRPIECE/TOUPEE MAINTENANCE

If you wear a hairpiece/toupee (or now called a "hair system"), make sure you check it for a few typical problems to keep it looking as good as it can.

First of all, make sure the color is the color of real hair. Real hair is a combination of many shades of whatever your real hair color is. For example, dark hair is a combination of different shades of reds and browns. A lot of hairpieces have the one color look. That is a major give away that you are wearing a hairpiece.

When shampooing your hairpiece, make sure to use a shampoo that is made for color treated hair. It will say so on the label. This will help the hairpiece retain its color longer so the hair won't have a dull, washed out look.

Make sure you wear one that was made recently! The old style hairpiece looks like a hairpiece, and you'd most likely look better without it.

If you wear a hairpiece or are thinking of wearing one, go for the best quality, which usually means the more expensive one. After all, the idea of wearing one is to improve your appearance. Wearing a cheap looking hairpiece will not make you feel better about yourself.

If you decide to wear a hairpiece it is something that requires monthly upkeep. You have to go and have it professionally cleaned and checked for hair replacement. It is certain that the hair will fall out of it over time. That hair needs to be replaced. It can be a costly investment to wear a hairpiece and keep it looking good. Keep this in mind if you're someone thinking about wearing one.

Here are a few styling tips that will keep your hairpiece looking as natural as it can.

First of all, when styling it, having the hair fall in the front will look better. If you comb it back chances are you will expose the ridge or border of the hairpiece and it will be obvious you are wearing one. Even the more recent hair systems have trouble disguising the front border. Also, when styling your hair and your hairpiece make sure you don't have the "helmet" look. This means that if the hairstyle looks too perfect and the hair doesn't move in the wind (like real hair does) it is another sign that you are wearing a hairpiece. I'm sure you've seen guys whose hair looked too perfect and glued down and you've said to yourself that it must be a hairpiece. If you have the kind of hairpiece that is bonded (meaning it stays on until you go in to have it taken off and cleaned) after you blow dry it, spray it with a moisture spray that is made for hair. You can find one of these sprays at any beauty supply store. Sometimes the salon where you go to have your hairpiece serviced sells products for the hair, including a moisture spray. A moisture spray will give it a more natural shine. Another trick to making your hair look natural is to use a light hair spray on it or a spray gel that has a super shine. The shine will give it a natural shimmer that real hair has. Also, make sure that whoever cuts and styles the hairpiece blends it in with your real hair. There should not be an obvious difference from where the hairpiece ends and your real hair beings. Don't leave the salon unless you like how it looks. Tell the stylist to keep work on it until you're totally satisfied. Don't be afraid to ask a friend to tell you the truth on how good, or not good it looks!

Another good styling tip is to take a fine-toothed comb and gently comb out the hairs in the front. This will keep them separated and looking more natural. Sometimes the glue from the tape or glue can get "gooey" and the comb helps to keep the hair separated from the glue. If you get glue into the front of the hair, spray some rubbing alcohol (try to find one that has a 99% alcohol instead of 70%) on your comb and then comb the front to help dissolve the glue. Don't overuse the alcohol as it can alter the color of the hair over time.

For those of you who are wearing a hairpiece and are thinking about going "natural", I say GO FOR IT! It can be scary to think of not wearing one. You may be afraid you're not going to be attractive or desired without it. The truth is you may look much better without it, and your dating life is just as good or actually gets better! I know someone who wore an excellent looking hairpiece for years and was afraid to just simply shave his head. He finally went "natural" and to his surprise his dating life skyrocketed!

If you choose to wear or keep wearing your hairpiece, at least take the time and effort to make it look the best it can.

OPTIONS FOR COLORING YOUR HAIR

Some of you who have graying hair may be thinking about dying your hair. There are a few issues with dying your hair. The main issue is which color to choose. There are a lot of choices out there and you don't want to pick the "wrong" color, which usually means a color that is too dark or too light compared to what your real hair color is. If you are going for a change that's one thing, but most guys are trying to just cover the gray so their hair color looks like it used to. Hair dyes are typically made either as "permanent" or "semi-permanent." Permanent hair dyes are the most popular. Some people choose not to use hair dyes because they think they are toxic, which they are, since they contain harsh chemicals, which you leave on your scalp. However, the hair dye made by "Just For Men" is only left on your head for 5 minutes. So if you are going to go for it, try that one since you'll be less likely to absorb the toxins with just 5 minutes of the dye on your head. "Just For Men" also contains some vitamins, which help to condition the hair. Remember to do a "patch" test for allergies and a potential bad reaction before you apply the dye to your hair (directions for patch testing you'll find on the directions sheet inside the box). It's worth taking the time to do the patch test. It's tempting to just go ahead and go for it, but obviously you don't want to go ahead with it without knowing if you'll have a bad reaction.

Now let's get back to how to choose the right color. You want to get as close as possible to the hair color shown on the box to your own natural hair color. Sometimes it can be difficult to choose because your hair may look a little lighter or darker than the hair color shown on the box. If you're not sure what to do, going with the slightly lighter color will probably be your best bet. Remember, you're trying to cover the gray hair! So, going with a slightly lighter color than your own will typically blend better as hair color is made up of several different colors, and a slightly lighter color will blend better. If you decide to try the slightly darker color than your hair color, it may look more noticeable. (If you really screw up the color you can always go to a salon and have their colorist fix it, but most likely that won't be necessary!)

Before you get started make sure you get everything together that you need before you dye your hair. Time is of the essence, and you don't want to be fumbling around for a towel while the dye is dripping down your face. You'll need:

1. **Rubber gloves**. Most of the coloring kits come with a pair of gloves, but you can always purchase a few pair at any beauty supply store. This is a good idea just in case the gloves that come in the box get torn.

2. **A comb**. Not the one you normally use. For shorter hair, just using your fingers to swirl around the color is sufficient. But for medium to longer length hair, a comb will help distribute the color evenly through the hair.

3. **Old clothes**. Don't dye your hair without having as much of your skin covered as possible. The dye isn't exactly gentle on your skin and though you might be tempted to do this au natural, keep in mind that it's better to damage an old T-shirt than your skin.

4. **An old towel or paper towel**, for wiping off any excess dye from your forehead, neck, and ears. (Check regularly once the dye is on to wipe of any excess dye).

5. **A timer** (a clock will due as long as it's in view from the start!)

VERY IMPORTANT: READ THE DIRECTIONS ON THE BOX AT LEAST TWICE BEFORE YOU BEGIN. Different products have very different instructions. For example, some require your hair to be dry, and others wet.

A good tip is to rub some Vaseline around your hairline as a protective measure before applying color. To remove the Vaseline after coloring your hair, rub a small amount of cream cleanser and wipe it off with cotton balls. If you forgot the Vaseline and have stained your skin, rub the area with a cotton ball soaked in alcohol-based toner to remove the excess dye.

Once you have finished dying your hair remember to use a shampoo and conditioner that is made for color treated hair. This will keep the color in longer and prevent it from fading.

Another option to dying your hair is by using what's called a hair color rejuvenator. One that you could try is called "Youthair", which you can check out at www.nomoregray.com. Typically within a few weeks of using these types of products your gray hair will gradually come back to your natural color. A product like Youthair substitutes for the loss of melanin and this combined with your hair's protein restores the hair back to its natural color. Of course you have to apply the product daily, and then once you reach your desired color about twice a week to keep it up. So it requires a little more time than just dying your hair. These products do work if you're willing to wait a few weeks for the results and are willing to do the maintenance.

Whichever technique you use to color your hair, it can make a positive difference in your appearance once you get the color to where it should be.

HOW TO HAVE THICKER LOOKING HAIR

Millions of men have thinning hair. So many spend a small fortune on products and even procedures that don't work! However, there are a few things you can try at home that may make a difference depending on how thin your hair is. Remember to be realistic. If you have hair that is thinning a lot, don't expect miracles from these products. These products work best on thinning hair, not on bald spots or a head that is basically bald.

One type of product that may help is called a hair thickener. Some product lines even have a shampoo, conditioner, and leave in product all designed to make your hair thicker, which will in turn make your head of hair look fuller. The good news is some of these products do work. However, keep your receipt, if you find it doesn't work for you return it for a full refund!

One product that I have seen really work well is called "Toppik" powder—which you can check out at toppik.com. Here's how it works when you apply it to your head. In seconds, thousands of tiny color matched hair fibers will intertwine with your own hair. Charged with static electricity, they bond so securely that they are supposed to stay in place all day and night.

The way it works is you order the color that comes closest to your hair color. Then, you simply sprinkle the product on your head, almost as if you're salting your head. The trick is to gently tap the bottle so that only a little bit of it comes out while moving the bottle over the thinning area so that it is evenly distributed. The Hair Building Fibers transform your thin, colorless "vellus" hairs. These "peach fuzz" type hairs becomes thick and full. In fact, your thinnest, limpest strands of hair are supposed to become so thick that even the thinnest areas look full again. I have seen this work and it really does a good job! The only thing is, it does shampoo out. So you have to reapply it every time you wash your hair. It also comes in a few different sizes, and the small bottle is great for travel or to just give it a try to see if you like it. Give Toppik a try before trying anything else and remember to be realistic with how full your hair will look.

Keeping your hair short and going a shade lighter than it is will also help your hair to look thicker.

HEALTHY TEETH

Everyone wants healthy, white teeth. From what I have found, here is the best way to accomplish that without harsh chemicals and dangerous procedures.

Don't use toothpaste! I know that's a shock, but most toothpaste at the market is sold with chemicals, fluorides, dyes, etc., that are actually harmful to your teeth. I stumbled across what's called tooth soap! Yes, a soap that cleans your teeth, which instead of harming your teeth and gums, actually promotes teeth/gum health. This concept was first talked about by Dr. Gerard F. Judd, PhD, author of *Good Teeth, Birth to Death;* and by Dr. Robert O. Nara, who dedicated his life to dentistry, and who also agrees with Dr. Judd about the use of a soap instead of a paste for teeth.

If you use toothpaste, you may be coating your teeth with contaminating materials that prevent good re-enamelization/re-mineralization. The only way your teeth can be strong and decay resistant is if you have clean teeth, which results in the enamel restoring itself. The best way to get clean teeth is to use tooth soap. I personally like the tooth soap at www.perfect-prescription.com. I am not affiliated with them in any way. I just like the tooth soap they make and they are very educated about why it's better to use tooth soap over toothpaste! At least check it out and educate yourself about it. You'll be glad you did and so will your teeth.

If you want to buy "tooth soap" at a health food store, you can buy a product called Pure Castile Soap. It's a liquid and basically has the same ingredients as the tooth soap sold at www.perfect-prescription.com. The one I use says on the label "Pure Castile Soap with oils of peppermint, olive and coconut, plus pure aloe vera." My teeth are extremely clean and I have very little plaque like I used to have when I used a typical toothpaste. If you still choose to use toothpaste, at least go for an all-natural one (Weleda makes great natural toothpaste in several flavors) to keep the chemicals out of your system. I recently went to the dentist after a year of not going and she was amazed how clean and healthy my teeth were! It has to be because of the tooth soap!

I want to briefly mention how you can keep your teeth sparkling white without the use of chemicals, and without spending a lot of money. You can simply use a tooth brightener like the one from perfect-prescription.com, which is all-natural, and will keep your teeth looking great. It's made from whole food calcium/magnesium and bicarb of soda. I am very happy with the results because my teeth look great!

Another item that is a must is what's called a "VIOlight." A VIOlight is a round cup like machine that sanitizes your toothbrush. It can destroy up to 99% of the bacteria living in your toothbrush! Since I started using it I don't wake up anymore with "gunk" all over my teeth. It can hold up to 4 toothbrushes. The light comes from a germicidal UV bulb that you turn on by pressing a button.

Just do a search for it, or you can go to www.violight.com to find out more. It really works great on keeping your toothbrush sanitized, which in turn keeps your teeth and mouth cleaner and more resistant to disease.

FINDING YOUR OWN STYLE

Finding your own style is perhaps one of the most challenging areas for men when it comes to choosing which clothes to wear. Some guys have a natural sense of what their style is, what look they like, which clothes/styles make them look their best, etc. They're the lucky ones when it comes to this topic! Then there are those guys, maybe even you, who don't pay much attention or don't even know what their "style" is! They just pick out whatever a friend or salesperson suggests, or maybe what they see in a magazine, or the basic colors that just kind of blend in with everyone else. When asked "what's your style" most guys don't have an answer! You can and should express your own style whether you work in a corporate environment or a casual one. You may be thinking, "That sounds great, but how?" There are several ways in which you can find your own style. First of all, if you don't already do this, try going clothes shopping on your own. The reason is it's important to take your time while shopping. You don't want anyone going with you who's going to rush you or suggest styles that they like, that they think you should wear until you know what your style is!

When you look at the different options of clothing try to determine what's calling to you. Forget about what you think you "should" wear. Try to determine for example, if the white shirt or the light blue shirt appeals more to you. Does the striped shirt or the pink shirt appeal to you? It sounds simple, but if you have that "don't care" attitude it may take you some time to figure out what YOU really like. It's kind of like stepping "out of the box" when it comes to buying your clothes. Believe it or not, clothes can make you feel better about yourself IF you are wearing something you really like.

Let's talk about shirts as an example. You're at the store and you want to find a few casual t-shirts to wear with jeans. There are a myriad of choices out there (if you're not in a store that has a lot of choices go to one that does!) I'd like you to gather a pile of casual t-shirts that are each different from the other. Solid colors, striped ones, funky ones, fun ones, even ones that you wouldn't think are for you! Let's assume that since you're at the store trying to find t-shirts to wear with jeans that you already have a pair of jeans on! Now go to the dressing room and try on each t-shirt. You will find that certain ones will look great on you and give you a good feeling, and certain ones will not. The ones that YOU like and give YOU a good feeling are obviously the ones that you should go with! You'll be surprised to find that the funky t-shirt with the fun decal on it is the one that appeals to you. The same goes for dress shirts. Don't assume you know what's going to look good on you. Try on several different shirts and styles to find out. If you haven't done this exercise before, try it on a bunch of different styles, and you will certainly find the shirts that are "you." I know from my own experience of someone telling me that a particular style wasn't going to look good on them. Then when they tried it on, they realized it did! Once you have experience trying on many different styles you will find your "own" style! Even if you have to dress a certain way for work, you can express your own style with a pair of fun socks or even a funky tie. It's great (and fun) to dress in a way that expresses who you are.

Since we're talking about trying on clothes, I want to remind you that wearing the right size is just as important as finding the style that appeals to you. Designers cut their clothes differently. If you're used to wearing a large, a large by one designer may fit you, whereas a large by another designer may be too small on you. If you like the shirt, try on the X-Large if the large doesn't fit. Don't get caught up in the size, if the shirt looks great on you, get the larger size. Who's going to know you're wearing an X-Large instead of a large? Remember, unless you're in great shape, going with a larger size will typically make you look thinner. If you have a belly, you don't want to accentuate it.

The same goes for pants. Although pants are pretty typical in terms of colors, there are many different cuts (pleated front, flat front, slim cut, stretch waist, etc.) The only way you'll be sure what you like, and what looks best on you, is by trying on the different choices and then you'll know! Again, it sounds simple, but I know for a fact that a lot of guys haven't taken the time to do this, and when they do, they realize it was worth taking the time to do it. Remember with pants, the length should fall just below your heel and the waist should not be tight. A tight waist with a tucked in shirt will make you look heavier and will be uncomfortable to wear. Keep this in mind when buying pants.

One more aspect of finding your own style I want to mention is to be aware of material. There are several different types of materials out there. For example, 100% cotton, some form of a cotton/polyester blend, polyester, silk, linen, wool, rayon, etc. Be aware if there is a particular fabric that appeals to you. Most guys like 100% cotton because it is typically more comfortable and "breathes" more than other fabrics. Again, it's a personal choice but once you're aware of the different fabrics to choose from that will also play a part in what you pick out. Also be aware that certain fabrics require dry cleaning only. If dry cleaning is something you don't want to bother with due to cost or health issues, make sure to check the label for washing instructions.

Once you find YOUR style, shopping for clothes becomes a different experience because you can hone in on the styles you know you like, and before you know it you'll be expressing yourself through your clothes and you will find your own style!

The next section will help you with figuring out what to wear!

WHAT TO WEAR

Wearing the right clothes is also an important aspect to the way you look. Of course everyone has their own style, and depending on what you do to make your living, depends on if you're wearing a suit to work, or jeans and a t-shirt. However, there are a few important tips to keep in mind regardless of if you're wearing a suit or t-shirt and jeans.

First of all dress age appropriate. If you're over 30 and still wearing tight t-shirts and tight jeans like you did when you were younger STOP doing that! Nothing looks as bad as a guy dressing like he's a teenager when he's not! The truth is you will look better dressed in your real size with age appropriate clothes. Even if you're going out to a bar or club and you're trying to impress someone with your hot body, wearing something too tight will do the opposite. It gives you the "he's trying too hard" look! Also, make sure the hem of your pants falls just above the heel of your shoe whether you're wearing jeans or slacks. There's no flood coming! If you're not sure what size you truly are, go into any department store and ask the salesperson. They will tell you what size you are in both shirt size and your waist size. It's amazing how many guys that are a "medium" are wearing shirts marked "small", and guys that are really a "large" wearing shirts marked "medium." If you've gained a few pounds over the years, wearing a loose shirt will make you look and feel thinner. Don't be afraid to accept whatever size you are. Be proud of who you are and show it by dressing age appropriate and looking great! Keep in mind if your clothes are very wrinkled, take the few minutes it takes to iron that shirt and show everyone you come in contact with just how stylish you are!

Let's talk about what colors to wear. Typically if you have light skin and dark hair you're going to look better wearing shirts in white, black, red, navy, dark olive, burgundy and pink.

If you have light skin and lighter color hair (red, any shade of blond), you're going to look better wearing shirts in black, yellow, light blue, rust, turquoise and pink.

If you have dark skin, you're lucky in the respect that all colors will look great on you. However, white, red and yellow will be your best colors.

If you're not wearing the best colors for your skin and hair color, you will tend to have a washed out look.

Another troubled area to look out for is if you're wearing your waist too high up. You're waistline is not at your belly button! If you wear your pants too high up, it makes your body look out of proportion and it will age you. Typically you will see older guys doing this. So, if you're not an older guy or if you are, double check where you're wearing your waistline and make sure it's in the right place!

So you're heading to the beach or pool and you pull out that old bikini type bathing suit without trying it on to see how it fits this year. Like it or not, your body is always changing, so, that bathing suit may not fit like it did a year ago. If you are in excellent shape and ONLY if you are in excellent shape you can get away with wearing a bikini type bathing suit (a/k/a Speedos!) If you are slightly overweight or overweight please wear a bathing suit that will flatter your body. A good type of suit to wear would be a pair that looks like a pair of shorts. Typically a pair that comes down half way between your thigh and knee would be appropriate. So, before you head out to the beach, try on your current bathing suit and look in the mirror! Does it really look good on you? Is it flattering your particular body? If you're not sure, go out and buy a different more flattering bathing suit!

When it comes to shoes—we all have our different likes and dislikes regarding the style. One thing that says a lot though is what condition your shoes are in! Your shoes should be CLEAN and SHINY at all times! It makes a huge difference and people notice. Typically you should have a black and brown pair of comfortable shoes. Make sure they are made well. A well made shoe will help prevent back pain and cushion your step, which keeps your joints healthier. Even sneakers should be kept clean and as free of scuffs as possible. Take the time to get your shoes shined or do it yourself by buying a shoeshine kit. The few minutes it takes will be well worth it. Once you have a few pair of long lasting, "good" shoes, you'll really appreciate the difference. A good quality shoe will typically be more expensive than a cheaply made shoe. It is well worth the cost and they will last for years.

THE TRAVELING MAN

We all travel throughout the year for business and/or pleasure. Whether you go away for a weekend, week, or a month, you need to know the basics of how to pack grooming essentials.

First of all there are a few things to consider. If you are already using skin care products you have to decide if you're going to bring the whole jar/tube or just a portion of it. If you're going away just for a few days, or even a week, you should get yourself small plastic travel bottles/tubes. You can usually find a kit that contains several different sizes at your local pharmacy. Sometimes the kit even comes with labels so you can write what the product is and stick it on the appropriate bottle.

Once you have your travel size bottles, simply take your cleanser for example and pour just the amount you'll think you'll need into the travel size bottle. Do this for your other skin care products as well. This way you don't have to pack the large bottles or tubes, just the small travel size, which leaves more room in your suitcase for your clothes! Some skin care lines sell travel size kits. These are great for short trips. Just make sure to get the kit that is for your particular skin type (as discussed in the skin care section).

When it comes to what to pack for your shaving routine, that all depends on what products you use. If you use a shaving cream that comes in a can, you can try to find a travel size can. Chances are you won't find a travel size can, and you'll have to bring the full size with you. However, if you use a shaving gel, you can for sure squeeze out some gel into a travel size tube and just bring that with you. If you're someone who uses a shaving brush, with a shaving soap, simply pack the shaving soap with the brush in a zip lock bag and you're all set. When it comes to bringing your aftershave along, if it's in a large jar/tube, put some in a travel size container to save space in your suitcase.

Shower gels, shampoos and conditioners that come in large bottles have no place in your suitcase. Even if you have to buy more travel size tubes, transfer your shower gel, shampoo and conditioner each into their own bottle. You don't want to get to your location and have a counter full of full size products when you're only going to be there a short time. When all your travel size bottles and/or jars are filled and securely closed, simply put them all in a large zip lock bag. This will keep your clothes protected should something leak. If you have a small travel bag for such items that fits inside your suitcase, put them in there for safekeeping. Just make sure that it is lined in plastic so that if something spills out it won't leak into your suitcase. I can't stress enough to make sure NOT to just throw all your travel sized bottles or jars into your main suitcase. The last thing you want is to arrive somewhere with stains all over your clothes from something that leaked out of a bottle or tube. For those of you who wear cologne, make sure to put your cologne bottle into a small zip lock bag as well in case of a spill.

If you're not sure how much of a particular product you will need, to play it safe, simply fill the entire travel size bottle with whatever it is you'll need. It's better to have some left over than to run out of something far from home.

Whatever grooming products you use, keep them all together when you get to your destination. That way, you don't have to waste time looking for a particular product. I like to have all my travel size bottles in a small travel tote so that I always know where the products are.

If you're going to a destination that has a different climate than where you're coming from, make sure to have the appropriate skin care products with you. For example, if you're going from a cold climate to a very hot climate, you don't need the same heavy moisturizer you would use in a cold climate. All you would need is a very light moisturizer that is appropriate for a warmer climate. Make sure to keep that in mind when packing. If you're going to a climate that is very tropical where there are a lot of bugs, make certain that whatever moisturizer you are using has no fragrance that will attract bugs.

Another great item to have on hand when traveling, are individually wrapped hand wipes. These come in handy should you not have access to napkins and you need to wash your hands or face.

The whole idea of being prepared when you travel is to make the trip as enjoyable and easy as possible. Keep all the above ideas in mind and have a great time!

GROOMING TIPS WHILE ON A DATE

When you're on a date (or business lunch/dinner, etc.) there are a few things you want to check during the date to make sure you're at your best! First of all I'm sure I don't have to remind you, but I'm assuming you've checked the "Top 4" before you leave home so you're looking your best!

When you go out to dinner with your date (or even if it's at home) half way through the meal, excuse yourself from the table and go to the men's room.

You're not going because you have to pee!

You're going to check on a few things. First, you're going to check your teeth! There's nothing more unappealing than talking with someone (or thinking of kissing someone) who has food stuck in their teeth! So, check for food stuck in your teeth and if there is any, get it out! Also, check for any eye lashes, hair, or crumbs that may have fallen on your face (this happens so check!), and while you're at it check for that eye "gook" that gets in the corners of the eye and remove it if it's there. Also, check your shirt and pants to make sure there are no crumbs and/or food on your clothes.

After you've made sure all is "clear", you (and your date) will be glad you went the extra mile to make sure your grooming was in check!

While you're in the men's room, check your hair and make sure it looks like you want it to look.

If you have oily skin, remember the oil blotting sheets I talked about in the skin care section? Make sure to bring a few with you and blot your nose and forehead (and if you're bald, the bald area too) to keep the shine away.

Another good idea is to keep mints or a breath spray on you so at the end of the meal you can freshen your breath and be confident that you're kissable.

Taking the few minutes it takes to check for these things will keep your confidence level up too, knowing that you're looking great, and that confidence will make you very appealing!

HOW TO LOOK YOUR BEST IN PHOTOGRAPHS

Whether you are posing for a professional picture or just casually for a friend, you SHOULD know what your best look is.

I'm not talking about a particular "pose", but I am talking about the way you position yourself. You may think, "what's the difference, I stand there and someone takes a picture." Well, there is a big difference when you know you have what I call your "camera look" and you did your best to look great in the picture.

Your "camera look" is the look you'll have after practicing the techniques below. Remember, pictures last FOREVER! You don't want to be one of those people who you see in pictures that look dazed and confused. Whether it's for a friend, a fancy affair, or for a professional photographer, years from now you'll be glad you did your best at the time.

The way to find out what your best "camera look" is to stand in front of a mirror and practice! You should know your best look when you smile, and your best look without smiling. Of course, usually you will smile for a picture. So, in front of your mirror, smile wide, smile just a little, smile with your lips open, with your lips closed, smile with your lower jaw relaxed, and with you're your teeth clenched together. Check to make sure your forehead is relaxed to avoid unnecessary forehead lines in the picture. Another trick is to press the tip of your tongue against the roof of your mouth or press the sides of your tongue against the roof of your mouth. This will tighten your neck below your chin. Try it and see if you like what it does for you. Also, try slightly sucking in your cheeks towards your tongue. This gives a lot of guys a more slimming, chiseled look in the face.

Try ALL the above combinations! Pick your favorite and use it when someone is taking a picture of you. After you find the look you like, you'll be happy to say "sure" when someone says, "let's take a picture!" Another trick of the trade is if possible to have the person taking the picture take it from a higher point than you are. This will give your face a more "chiseled" look as well.

One more tip to help you not "blink" during a picture with a flash is to ask the photographer to count to three. On the counts of one and two keep your eyes closed. At the very beginning of the count of "three", open your eyes. This will usually prevent your eyes from closing with the flash.

With a little practice, you'll get your "camera look" down and you can have your picture taken with confidence.

Try all the suggestions above until you find one or two looks you like the best. Of course I know you're doing the "Top 4" so you'll look your best at all times. For those of you with oily skin, make sure to excuse yourself and find a place where you can quickly use your oil blotting paper so your skin won't be shiny in the picture.

When you see your picture, you'll be glad you took the time to find your "camera look."

HOW TO WALK SO YOU LOOK YOUR BEST

You may be surprised that I'm asking you to focus on how you walk. However, it's VERY important to be aware of. After all, most of us have been walking around having no idea what our feet are doing. Take a short walk and notice if your feet are straight when you walk or if one foot is turned to the right or left, while the other foot is straight. Or, are both feet turned out when you walk? If so, you have to re-train yourself to walk as if both feet are following a straight line. This will improve your overall look in general and when you are approaching someone. This will take practice because you are used to walking a certain way. The trick is to remind yourself as much as possible every day while you are walking to be aware of how you are walking! In time you can correct a "sloppy" walk and you'll be glad you did! This is one of those tips that seem like no big deal, but it's a huge deal to people that see you! It's always a plus to be aware of something you just take for granted, like walking. Also, make sure when you walk that you are walking with confidence, head held high, shoulders relaxed, back straight, not slouched. With practice and patience you can learn to turn your sloppy walk into a graceful, confident walk.

EXERCISE AND HEALTHY EATING

As part of keeping yourself looking and feeling your best, I am going to recommend an exercise you may not know of. You can add this to your existing exercise routine, or if you're not exercising and you're looking for an easy, fun way to burn calories and do something good for yourself, try what's called Rebounding. Rebounding is when you exercise with what looks like a mini-trampoline. Of course if for some reason you are restricted from exercising, check with your doctor to make sure you can start using a rebounder. Most rebounders come with an attachable bar, which you can hold onto if you want to bounce while holding onto a bar to help you keep your balance.

Rebounding is not only the most efficient, effective form of exercise to help you burn fat, lose weight, and get in shape, but it is also good for your cells which is why I use it, and highly recommend it. Rebounding is a concentrated form of exercise that affects every cell in your body in a good way.

Moving and stretching a cell—as rebounding does—helps to supply nutrients and eliminate toxic waste. When you bounce on a rebounder, your entire body (internal organs, bones, connective tissue, and skin) becomes stronger, more flexible, and healthier. Both blood circulation and lymphatic drainage are greatly improved, which keep you healthy!

According to my research, the key benefits of regular rebounding are excellent and include the following:

- Burns Fat
- Helps Get Rid of Toxins
- Stronger bones and joints
- Improves circulation
- Improves immunity
- Faster healing
- Improves sagging skin
- Strengthens muscles
- Resolves back problems
- Lowers blood pressure
- Improves vision
- Improves hearing
- Decreases appetite
- Improves digestion
- Enhances brain function
- Eliminates tiredness

You can see from the above list how wonderful it is for you. If you want to try rebounding, make sure to buy the best. They are sold in all different price ranges, but the more expensive ones are made better and offer the best bounce and cushion, which makes it easier on your joints. This is one piece of exercise equipment that you DON'T want to save money on! For those of you that want an aerobic session with your rebounder you can buy rebounding exercise videos that will give you an excellent workout.

Healthy Eating:

Eating healthy is also paramount to looking your best. Research has shown that staying away from white sugar and processed foods while eating organic whole grains, protein, fruits and vegetables will keep you healthy and slim. It will also keep your skin glowing! Try to eat organic fruits, vegetables and meats, as they are much healthier for you. When buying meats (chicken, turkey, beef) try to buy hormone-free meats. Typically, you can find hormone free meats at your local health food market. If hormones are in the meats you eat, that means they're in your system too.

It can be hard to maintain a healthy diet all the time, but if you just start somewhere, for example, deciding to eat less of the bad stuff (i.e., white sugar, white flour) and more of the good stuff (i.e., organic fruits and vegetables), that alone is an amazing start. Also, drinking at least 50 oz. of pure water per day is excellent for keeping you healthy and your skin looking great.

The latest report from The Environmental Working Group shows the top 12 fruits and vegetables you MUST buy organic and which ones if you can't buy organic, are not as loaded with pesticides as the others.

The 12 Most Contaminated—Buy These Organic:

1. Apples
2. Bell Peppers
3. Celery
4. Cherries
5. Imported Grapes
6. Nectarines
7. Peaches
8. Pears
9. Potatoes
10. Red Raspberries
11. Spinach
12. Strawberries

12 Least Contaminated—Don't Need to Purchase Organic:

1. Asparagus
2. Avocados
3. Bananas
4. Broccoli
5. Cauliflower
6. Corn (sweet)
7. Kiwi
8. Mangos

9. Onions

10. Papaya

11. Pineapples

12. Peas (sweet)

There is also ONE oil out there that is AMAZING for your health (yes ONE) and is also great for your skin! It's coconut oil. Coconut oil is used as a base in many soaps and shower gels as well. I also want you to know of the many health benefits of coconut oil.

According to my research from those in "the know" (such as acclaimed scientist Raymond Francis at www.beyondhealth.com, Dr. Mary Enig, Dr. Bruce Fife, and even the book "The Coconut Oil Miracle" by Jon J. Kabara Ph.D.), coconut oil is becoming known as a miracle fat that: boosts energy, burns fat, is antibiotic, and helps with thyroid problems. Coconut oil has been safely used for thousands of years. Natives in tropical climates who consume lots of coconut oil don't suffer from heart disease, cancer, colon problems, and other health challenges that we do. Because it is highly saturated, coconut oil is very stable, stores well, and is suitable for cooking. But don't let the saturated fat in coconut oil bother you. These saturated fats are different. The medium-chain fatty acids in coconut oil are easy to absorb, digest, transport, and metabolize in the body. Unlike other saturated fats, the medium-chain fatty acids in coconut oil speed up the body's metabolism and are used by the body to produce energy rather than being stored as fat. Coconut oil does a body good. Here's what the scientists and doctors are saying:

Heart Healthy

Population studies show that coconut oil lowers cholesterol, and reduces risk of heart disease. Americans consistently have higher cholesterol levels than coconut eating cultures.

Weight Control

Coconut oil helps you to lose, maintain, or gain weight depending on your body's need. It contributes to weight loss by speeding metabolism and being used as fuel rather than stored as fat. For underweight people, coconut oil helps to gain weight, especially useful to those suffering from AIDS or cancer.

Infection Fighting

The medium-chain fatty acids and monoglycerides found in coconut oil are the same as those in human mother's milk, and they have extraordinary antimicrobial properties. By disrupting the lipid structures of microbes, they inactivate them. About half of coconut oil consists of lauric acid. Lauric acid, its metabolite monolaurin, and other fatty acids in coconut oil are known to protect against infection from bacteria, viruses, yeast, fungi, and parasites. While not having any negative effect on beneficial gut bacteria, coconut oil inactivates undesirable microbes such as H-pylori, Candida albicans, and Giardia. Natives in Southeast Asia who drink filthy water, loaded with bacteria and parasites, are nonetheless healthy, mostly due to the protective effect of the coconut oil in their diets.

Thyroid Support

Coconut oil helps people with low thyroid function. Regular oils such as soybean, canola, safflower and corn suppress thyroid function. The medium-chain fatty acids in coconut oil stimulate metabolism, boost energy, and promote weight loss. While not a cure, some people have been able to reduce and even eliminate their thyroid medications due to the benefits of eating coconut oil.

Cancer Protective

Coconut oil appears to protect against cancer and not to promote cancer. Animal studies have shown that when animals are fed carcinogens and a variety of oils, the animals that do not develop cancer are those on coconut oil.

Anti-Inflammatory Effects

Coconut oil appears to have anti-inflammatory effects. For the past 20 years it has been known that coconut oil has been beneficial to patients with inflammatory bowel diseases such as Crohn's disease. Coconut oil appears to have a direct effect in suppressing inflammation and repairing tissue, and it may also contribute by inhibiting harmful intestinal microorganisms that cause chronic inflammation.

Good for the Skin—(One of my favorite aspects!)

Coconut oil rejuvenates skin and wrinkles and slows the aging and wrinkling of skin. Used as a lotion, it protects against sun damage, and strengthens underlying tissues. It moisturizes, heals sores and injuries, and prevents production of "liver spots," (oxidized oils). When liver spots occur, this same oxidative damage is also happening in other tissues such as the brain, heart, eyes, and blood vessels.

Among other properties, coconut oil:

- Does not require refrigeration, and is stable at room temperature from one to five years;

- Increases lung function by increasing the fluidity of cell surfaces;
- Regulates blood sugar and prevents hypoglycemia by providing a supply of fuel not affected by insulin;
- Boosts energy in chronic fatigue and suppresses herpes and Epstein-Barr viruses; and
- Doesn't oxidize easily, thereby protecting the body from lipid peroxidation.

Virgin coconut oil is the least processed oil on the market. This extraordinary oil is not heated above normal air temperature, and it is made form freshly harvested coconuts. Most oils are made from copra (dried coconut), which can be contaminated with mold. Coconut oil is a sensible addition to anyone's diet. A therapeutic dose is three tablespoons a day. You can even spread some on a cracker or on toast to get your daily amount.

OTHER QUICK TIPS

- Sideburns. The rule for sideburns (if you don't want to make a statement with long side burns) is to trim them in line with the bridge of your nose. Using your eye, line up the bridge of your nose with your ear, and that's where your side burns should end. Also, make sure your side burns aren't too bushy. If they are, simply take a comb and at the bottom of the each side burn, comb up and take a scissor and trim the hair that pops up above the teeth of the comb to give them that well groomed look.
- If you're balding and you have a "comb over" thinking it's hiding the bald spot, and your part is down by your ear, you will look much better by cutting off the comb over and keeping the hair at the sides of your head cut very short. By having a comb over you are NOT hiding the fact that you are bald. You can also go for a shaved head look, which generally looks great. Make sure to go all the way by shaving your head with either an electric razor or with shaving cream and a disposable razor. You can also buy a special razor that's meant for shaving the head. It has a special groove for your fingers to glide it along the head for a smooth shave.

- What vitamins get rid of acne? Vitamin A and Zinc. Here's why. It has been proven that Vitamin A with carotenoids strengthens the protective tissue of the skin and prevents acne formation by reducing sebum production. Vitamin A is essential for the maintenance and repair of the tissue which the skin and mucous membranes are made of. Vitamin A is also a powerful antioxidant that relieves your body of oxidative stress caused by free radicals. Did you know that a deficiency in vitamin A could actually cause acne? It is recommended you take up to 10,000 IU of vitamin A a day to successfully combat acne. A high quality liquid multivitamin is a good source for vitamin A.

Zinc helps with healing of the tissues and helps prevent scarring. It helps prevent acne by regulating the activity of the oil glands. Zinc promotes a healthy immune system and the healing of wounds. It is also an antioxidant, which helps to fight and prevent the formation of free radicals. Acne can be a sign of a Zinc deficiency. The recommended dosage to fight acne is 25 to 30mg per day. If you are someone with acne, give this a try and you'll most likely be happy with the results in a few weeks.

- If you are tired when you get home from a long day and don't feel like going through the routine of cleansing your face, you can buy what's called a "toner." A toner is a liquid that you apply to a cotton ball and then you wipe it all over your face and neck, and it gets rid of all the grime. Make sure to get an alcohol-free toner, and once again get a toner for your skin type. If you try this, chances are you're cotton ball will look very dirty after you use it. You'll be amazed how much grime is on your skin! If your cotton ball is very dirty, saturate a new cotton ball and go over your face again for super clean skin.

- Fingernails and toenails. To complete your new look, make sure you trim your nails on your hands and feet. You can go out and get a manicure and pedicure, which has its benefits. Getting a professional manicure and pedicure keeps your nails growing in the right direction so you don't get an ingrown nail, and of course a professional will give them a great look. If you do get your nails professionally done, request that the manicurist buff your nails instead of using polish. Buffing lasts longer and looks great. If you get clear polish put on your nails, it starts to chip before you know it. Doing your own at home mini manicure and pedicure will also give you a nice look. When cutting the nails on your hand, use a good pair of nail clippers. Simply cut around the tip of the nail leaving only a small tip. Just make sure that each nail is even and clean. Nothing is as unattractive as seeing dirt under the nail, even if it's not a long nail. When trimming your toes also only leave a small tip. Using your nail clippers you can also open up the little attachment and pick out any lint from the sides of your big toes. If you have any dry skin on the heel of your foot, you can buy a pumice stone to smooth out the skin. Using a pumice stone is easy, just stick your feet in a shallow tub and while your feet are in the water take the pumice stone and gently rub it against the areas of the feet (usually the heels) that are ruff. When you're done, apply a moisturizer to your feet to soothe the skin.
- Sweaty Crotch. If you shower and in a short time have a sweaty crotch here's what you can try. Go to your local health food store and purchase a talc free body powder. After you shower and dry yourself off, apply a generous amount of powder to your crotch area. This will help absorb the excess moisture and control any odor. The powder will also keep your skin from rubbing together which

can cause a rash. Another technique you could try is to purchase an all natural under arm deodorant. After your shower and you're dry, apply to your crotch area and let it do its work. One of these methods will help you! Also, you may need to re-apply during the day. If you can purchase a small size bottle of what you like, you can keep it in your briefcase and re-apply as needed.

• Smelly socks and feet. If you suffer from smelly feet and socks get yourself a foot powder. It will take care of the odor so that when you're at your friend's house, or your house and you take off your shoes, you won't stink out the place! Trust me, if the odor is there and no one says anything you WILL be talked about when you leave!

• Check for eye "gook." You know how it is when you're talking with someone and you notice a big white piece of eye gook or crust in the corner of their eye! So, several times a day check for crust or gook in the corners of each eye. Usually if it's there, it's the corner of your eye closest to your nose. You want to keep the gook out so that no one has to notice it while you're talking to them!

• Eyeglasses. If you're still wearing those big aviator type glasses or big round oversized frames, guess what—they are way out of style! Get yourself a nice sleek small-framed pair of eyeglasses that fits your particular face. It will make you look younger and more modern. Go for small and sleek, not those dated aviator big-framed glasses. Better yet, if you haven't tried contact lenses give them a try. Contact lenses are now made softer and more comfortable than they used to be. If you already use contact lenses be sure to use an all-natural disinfecting solution like Clear Conscience Multi-Purpose Solution, which is Chlorhexidine free and Thimerosal free.

- Pee drops on the front of your pants. When you pee in a public restroom or at your home, make sure to take a small piece of toilet paper or a tissue with you! When you're done peeing, press the piece of toilet paper or tissue against the head of your penis and catch the last few dribbles of pee so they don't end up on the front of your pants. It's very common to have splattered pee on the front of your pants 90% of the time when you leave the bathroom. People notice and it's not appealing.
- Itchy skin after showering. If you tend to have itchy skin after you shower, chances are you need to stop using your current soap or shower gel and switch to one that is made with 100% glycerin. A glycerin soap or shower gel will leave your skin soft and rinses off easily. Most soap contains heavy animal fats or oils, which can tend to clog pores and irritate your skin. If you have allergies, asthma, skin problems and chemical sensitivities a pure (non-synthetic) glycerin soap will not irritate your skin. Another technique you can try is after your shower and you're dry, apply an all-natural moisturizer to your arms, legs, chest, and back. I also highly recommend the use of a filtered showerhead. A filtered showerhead will remove chlorine and other harmful skin irritants, leaving your skin soft and irritation free. A filtered showerhead will also leave your hair softer.
- Carry a mini Swiss army knife. Yes, that's right, carry one of those mini Swiss army knives at all times. Most of them have a little scissor that you can pull out. This scissor works great on trimming nose and ear hair. Say you're at the office and you go to the bathroom and you're washing your hands and you look in the mirror and you see a nose hair sticking out, or a long ear hair! Yikes! But you're prepared because you have your mini Swiss army knife. You take it out of your pants pocket, pull out the scissors and quickly cut

that nose hair or ear hair that was sticking out! Now you're ready to face the world again!

- Meditation does a body and mind good! It has been scientifically proven that meditation IS worth practicing. There are MANY different types of meditation. One of the easier and most effective meditations is called Vipassana meditation. I first discovered this in Los Angeles and studied with Vipassana master Shinzen Young. Shinzen not only received his Ph.D. in Buddhist studies, he had extensive training in Asia where he mastered several meditation traditions. (If you'd like to find out more about Shinzen Young and his practice visit www.shinzen.org). With Vipassana mediation, you simply observe the sensation of the breath going in and out of your nose. It's amazing what that does for you! It may sound easy, and it can be, but you'd be surprised what it takes to focus strictly on the breath. The reason why I am bringing it up in a book about grooming is because one of the benefits of meditation is it actually helps to decrease the appearance of fine lines and wrinkles. This happens because when you meditate every day, during the meditation your facial muscles become completely relaxed. In time, the relaxed muscles equal less noticeable fine lines/wrinkles. I have had friends tell me that they can notice when I meditate because my face looks more relaxed and I have a more youthful appearance. However, there are also some other excellent benefits to meditation. Here are just some of the other benefits you'll enjoy:

- Greater creativity.
- Decreased anxiety.
- Decreased depression.
- Decreased irritability and moodiness.

- Improved learning ability and memory.
- Increased self-actualization.
- Increased feelings of vitality and rejuvenation.
- Increased happiness.
- Increased emotional stability.

It has also been shown to help with:

- Deep rest-as measured by decreased metabolic rate, lower heart rate, and reduced workload of the heart.
- Lowered levels of cortisol and lactate-two chemicals associated with stress.
- Reduction of free radicals—unstable oxygen molecules that can cause tissue damage.
- Decreased high blood pressure.
- Higher skin resistance. Low skin resistance is correlated with higher stress and anxiety levels.
- Drop in cholesterol levels. High cholesterol is associated with cardiovascular disease.
- Improved flow of air to the lungs resulting in easier breathing. This has been very helpful to asthma patients.
- Decreases the aging process.
- Higher levels of DHEAS in the elderly. An additional sign of youthfulness.

With all these potential benefits—give it a try!!!

- Lips. Don't forget about your lips! Dry, cracked lips are not healthy for you, not to mention that they're very unappealing for the person looking at you! To keep your lips looking great, get yourself a natural lip quencher that has an SPF in it. Lips can get sun damaged too if not protected with an SPF. Use your lip quencher a few times a day to keep them moist and protected. Some will work better than others. You want to try to find one that isn't too shiny and that will actually keep your lips moist for several hours. A good lip quencher will have vitamin E, aloe and shea butter.

CONCLUSION

Now that you are fully informed with easy at home techniques on how to look your best (and ultimately feel your best), go for it—no more excuses!

Have fun experimenting with different skin care products, and all the other information you just learned.

Before you know it, you'll look great, feel great, you'll be more confident, and you'll even be giving advice to your friends and family about what they can do to look and feel their best!

I want to remind you to always keep in mind that it's all about looking YOUR personal best. You don't have to look like a male model to look great. It's all about taking care of your grooming needs and being confident in what you do.

Looking your best is a wonderful goal that can be achieved. Being the best person you can be, together with looking great, is even a better goal to achieve! I find that keeping a positive outlook on life, being good to yourself and others, also helps to give you a healthy glow from the inside out.

HELPFUL LINKS AND BOOKS

Helpful Internet sites that will help you improve not only your appearance, but your life as well:

(The author of this book is in NO WAY affiliated with any of the suggested sites listed below. They are strictly what the author believes will help you in your quest to look and be your best.)

www.beyondhealth.com—has some great information about eating healthfully and other health tips.

www.oprah.com—offers some great self-improvement techniques.

www.drbenkim.com—offers great advice on staying healthy.

www.jayrobb.com—offers great advice on losing weight.

www.roex.com—offers great information on what vitamins to take.

www.aboutface4men.com—offers great natural skin care for men.

www.4VOO.com—offers great natural skin care for men.

www.icelements.com—offers great all natural skin care.

www.lawofattractionbook.com—offers great advice on how to use the law of attraction to get the things you want in life.

HELPFUL BOOKS

Total Self-Confidence written by Dr. Robert Anthony

Never Be Sick Again written by Raymond Francis, M.Sc

Excuse Me Your Life Is Waiting written by Lynn Grabhorn

Seat Of The Soul written by Gary Zukov

Natural Cures They Don't Want You To Know About written by Kevin Trudeau

The Coconut Oil Miracle written by Bruce Fife, C.N., N.D.

The Secret written by Rhonda Byrne and guests

The Law of Attraction written by Michael Losier

Ask And It Is Given written by Esther and Jerry Hicks.

978-0-595-49311-1
0-595-49311-4

Made in the USA